AF393088

THIS BOOK BELONGS TO:

This book is the fruit of many practitioners' field research.
For any issues with your book, such as
faulty binding, printing errors, or something else.
Please, do not hesitate to contact us at: fajrour@gmail.com
We will make sure you get a replacement copy
immediately.

For any suggestions or questions regarding our books, Contact
us at: fajrour@gmail.com

Please, support us and leave a   review
Thank you!

I SPY with my smart eye, Something beginning with...

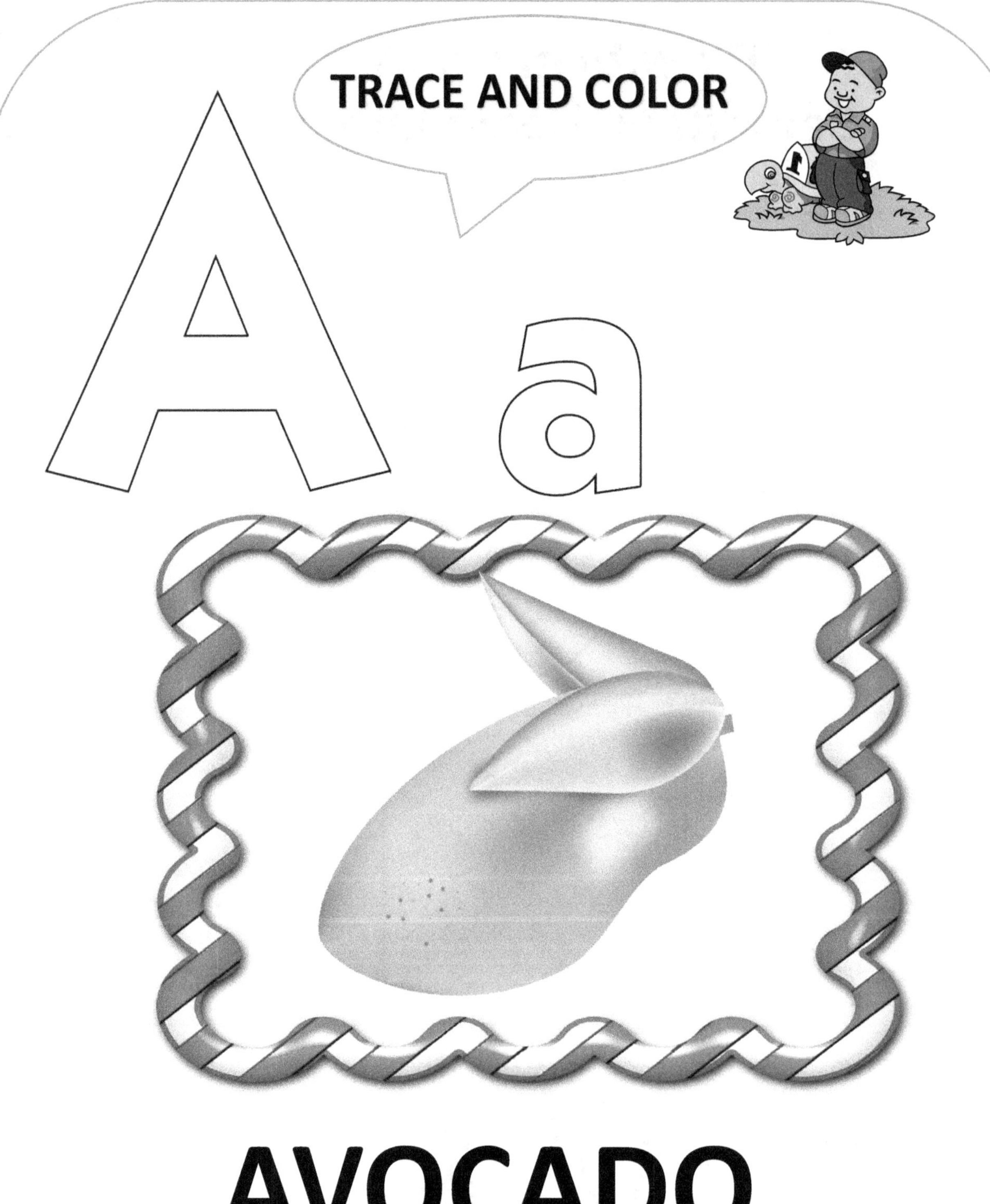

TRACE AND COLOR
A a
AVOCADO
avocado

I SPY with my smart eye,
Something beginning with...

BASKETBALL

basketball

I SPY with my smart eye,
Something beginning with...

C c

CHERRIES

Cherries

I SPY with my smart eye,
Something beginning with...
D d

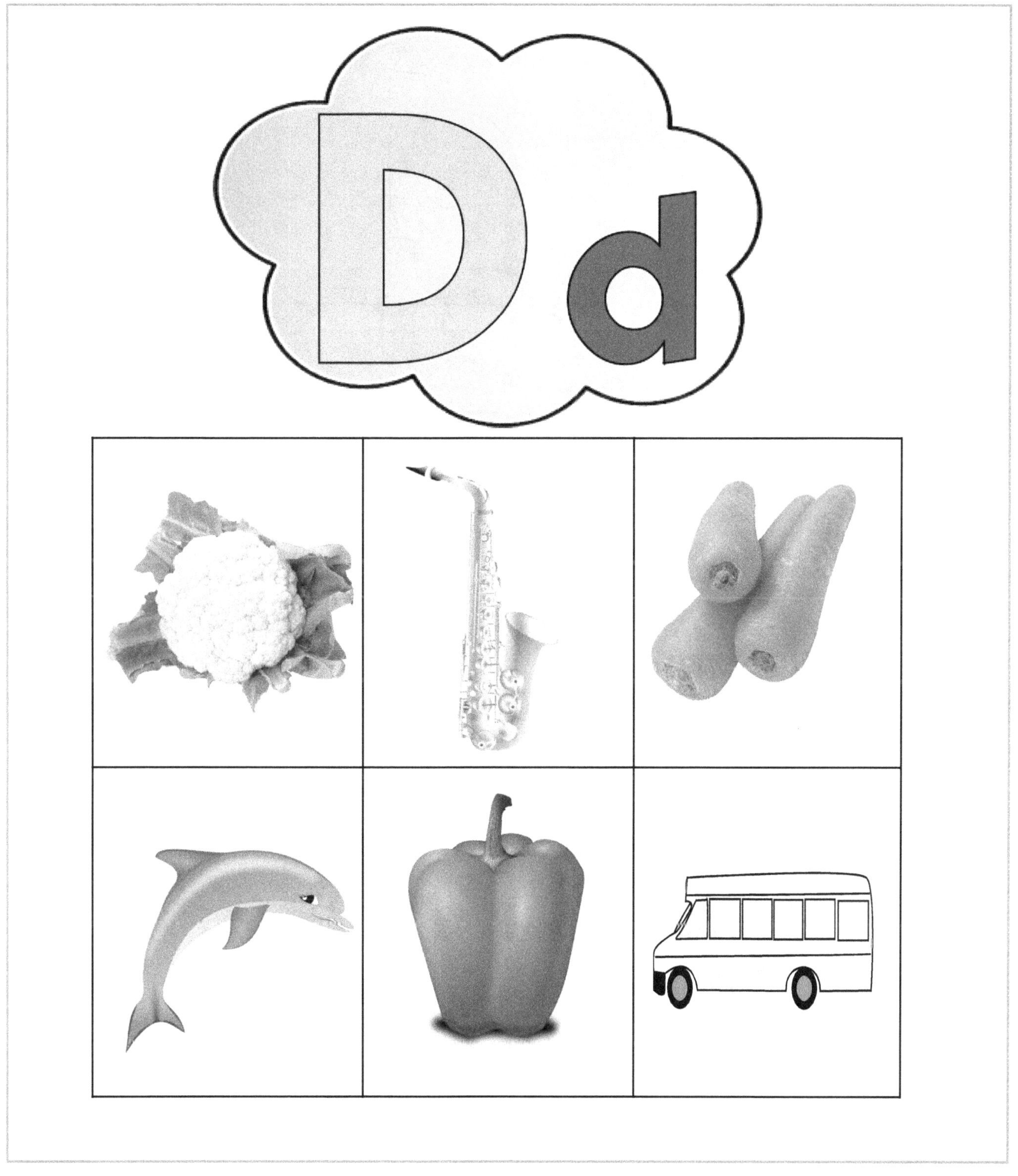

D d

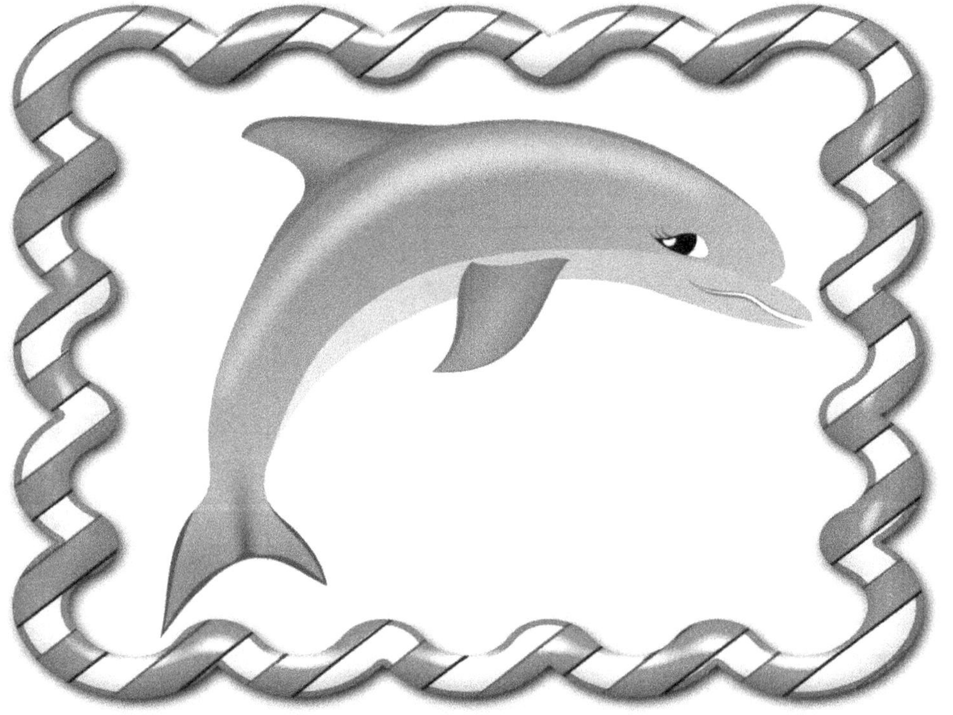

DOLPHIN

dolphin

I SPY with my smart eye,
Something beginning with…

E e

ELEPHANT

elephant

I SPY with my smart eye,
Something beginning with...

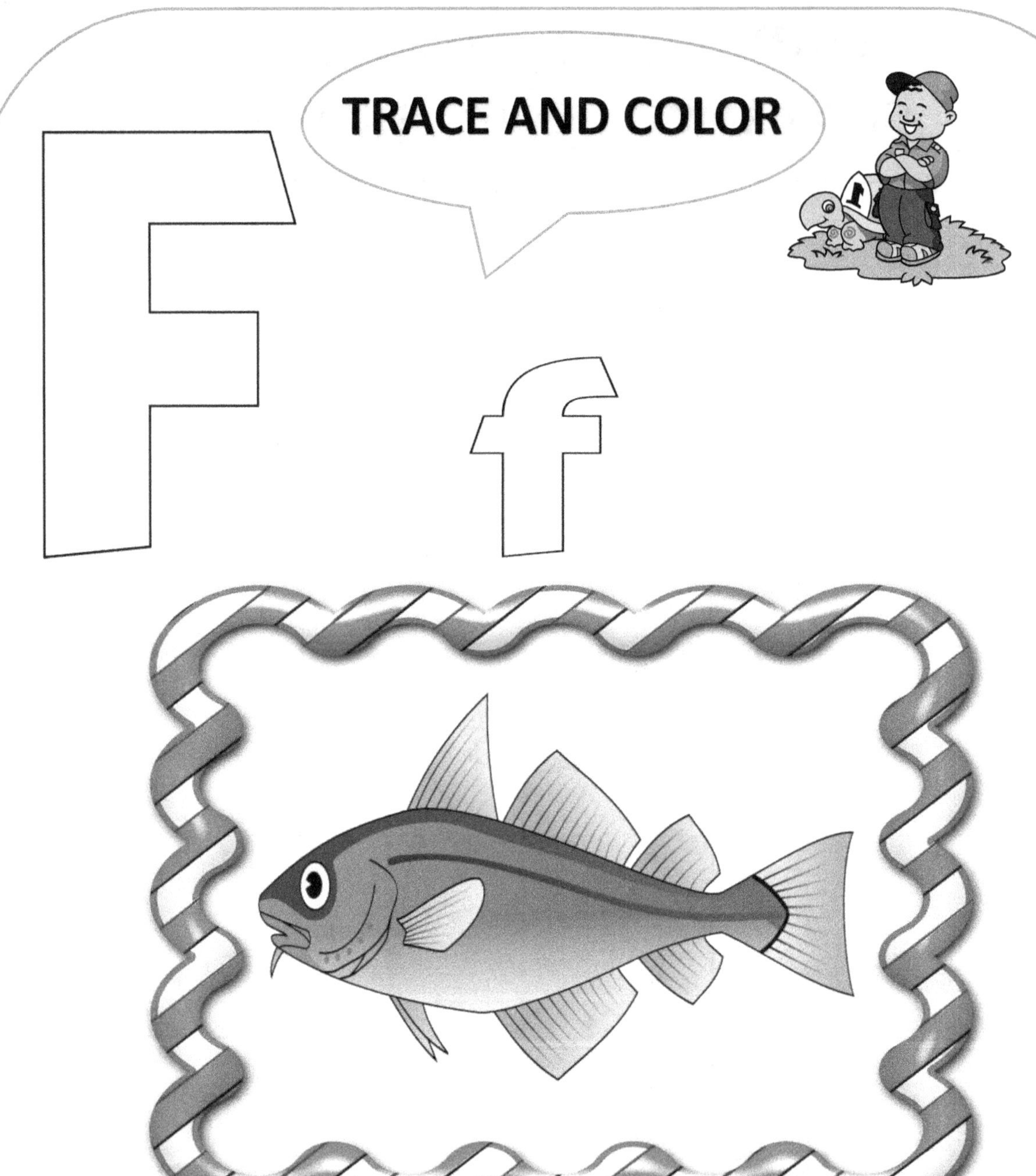

FISH

fish

I SPY with my smart eye,
Something beginning with...

G g

G g

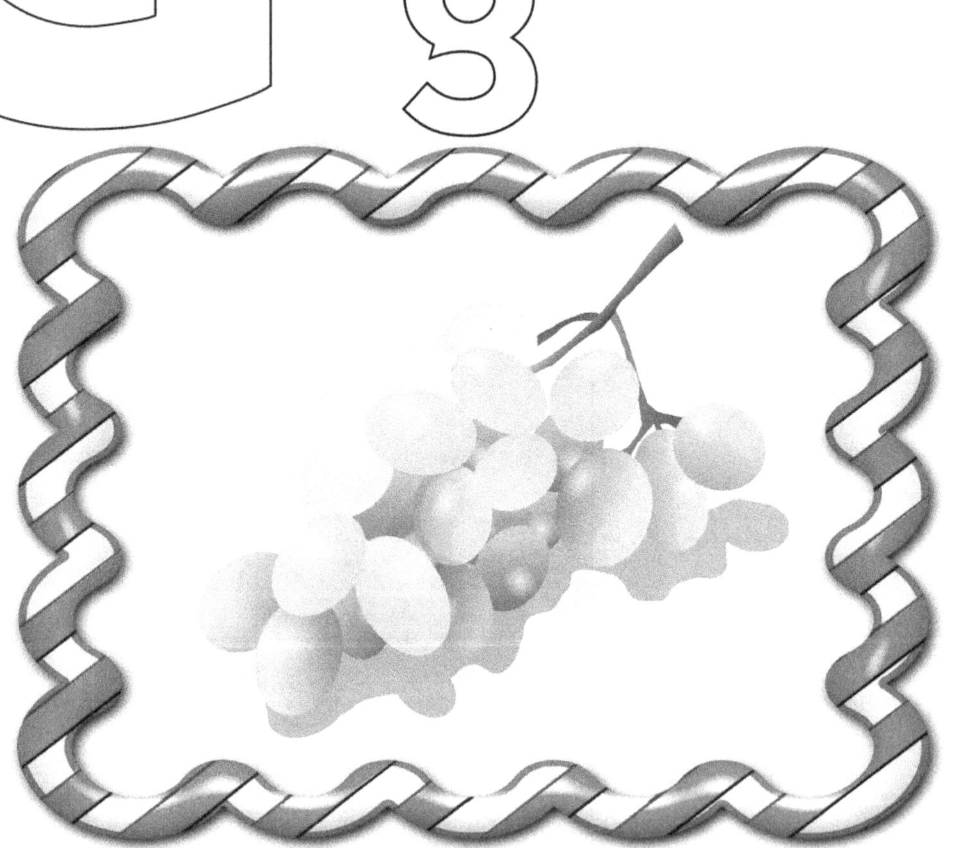

GRAPES

grapes

I SPY with my smart eye,
Something beginning with...

H h

H h

HERON

Heron

I SPY with my smart eye,
Something beginning with...

I i

ICE CREAM

ice cream

I SPY with my smart eye,
Something beginning with...

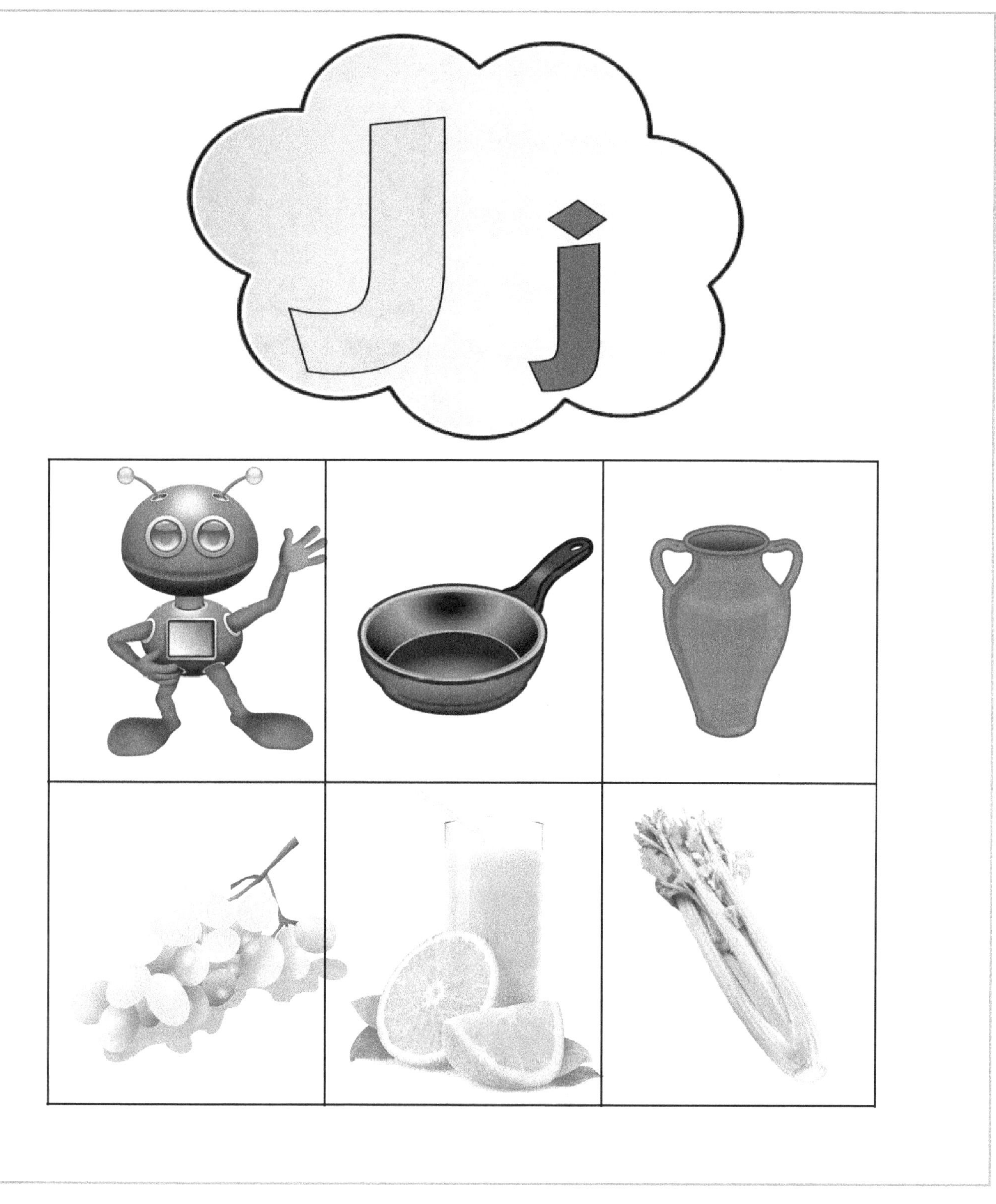

J j

JUICE
juice

I SPY with my smart eye,
Something beginning with...

K k

K k

KANGAROO

Kangaroo

I SPY with my smart eye, Something beginning with...

L l

LION

lion

I SPY with my smart eye,
Something beginning with...

MONKEY

monkey

I SPY with my smart eye, Something beginning with...

N n

NECTARINE

nectarine

I SPY with my smart eye,
Something beginning with...

ORANGE

orange

I SPY with my smart eye, Something beginning with…

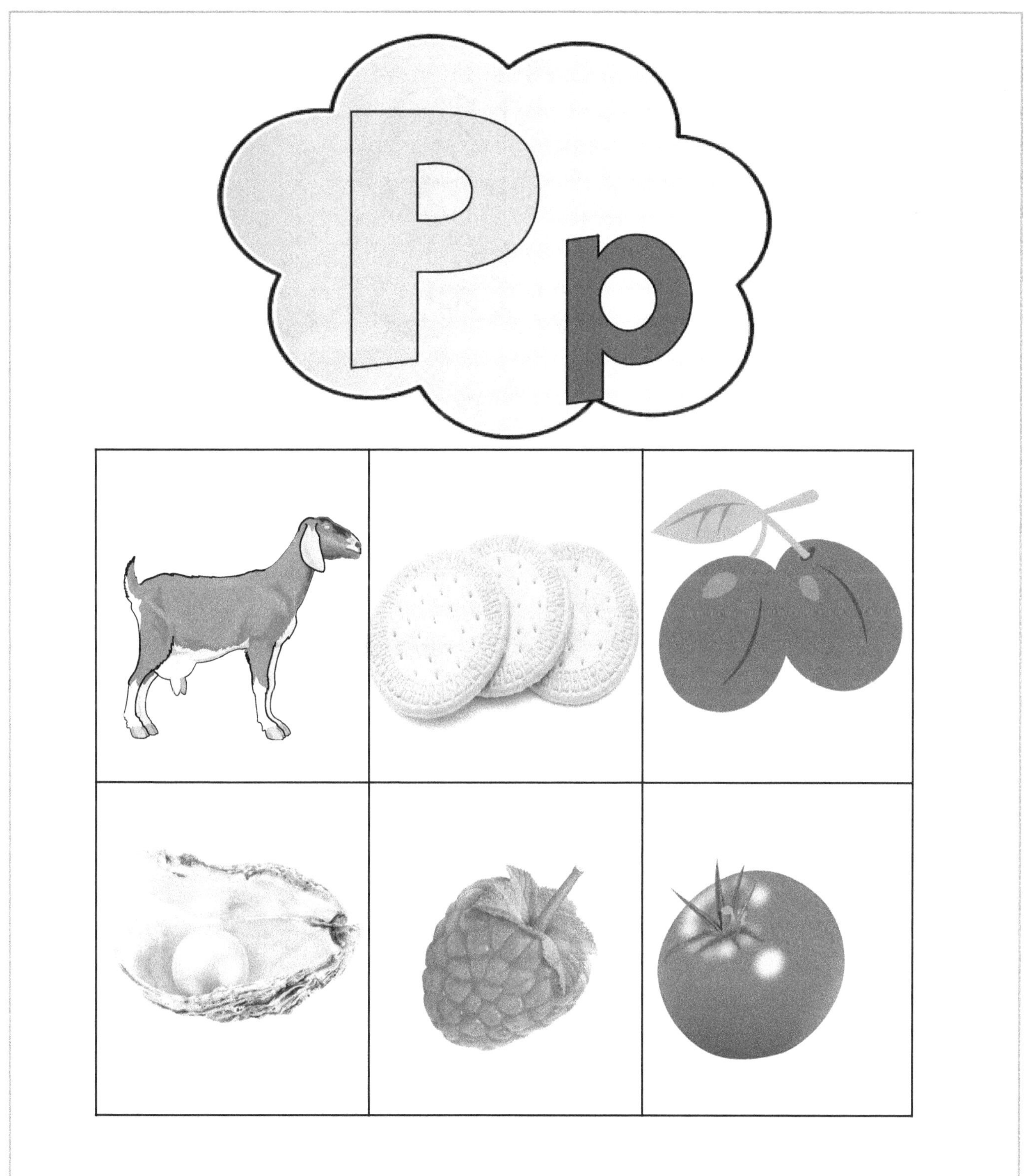

P p

PEARL

Pearl

I SPY with my smart eye,
Something beginning with…

QUINCE
quince

I SPY with my smart eye, Something beginning with…

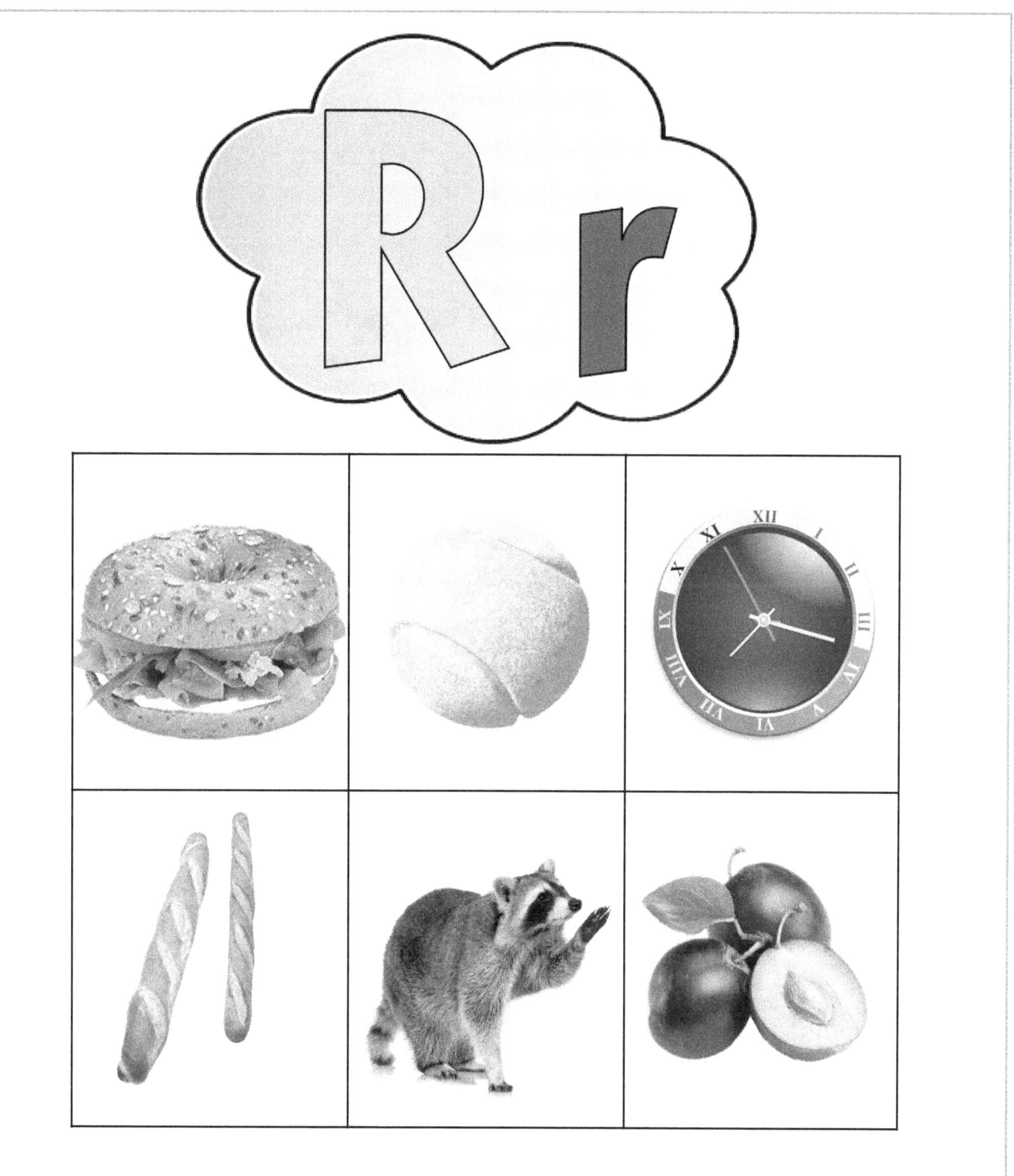

R r

RACCOON

raccoon

I SPY with my smart eye,
Something beginning with...

S s

SPINACH

spinach

I SPY with my smart eye,
Something beginning with…

T t

T t

TOMATO

tomato

I SPY with my smart eye,
Something beginning with...

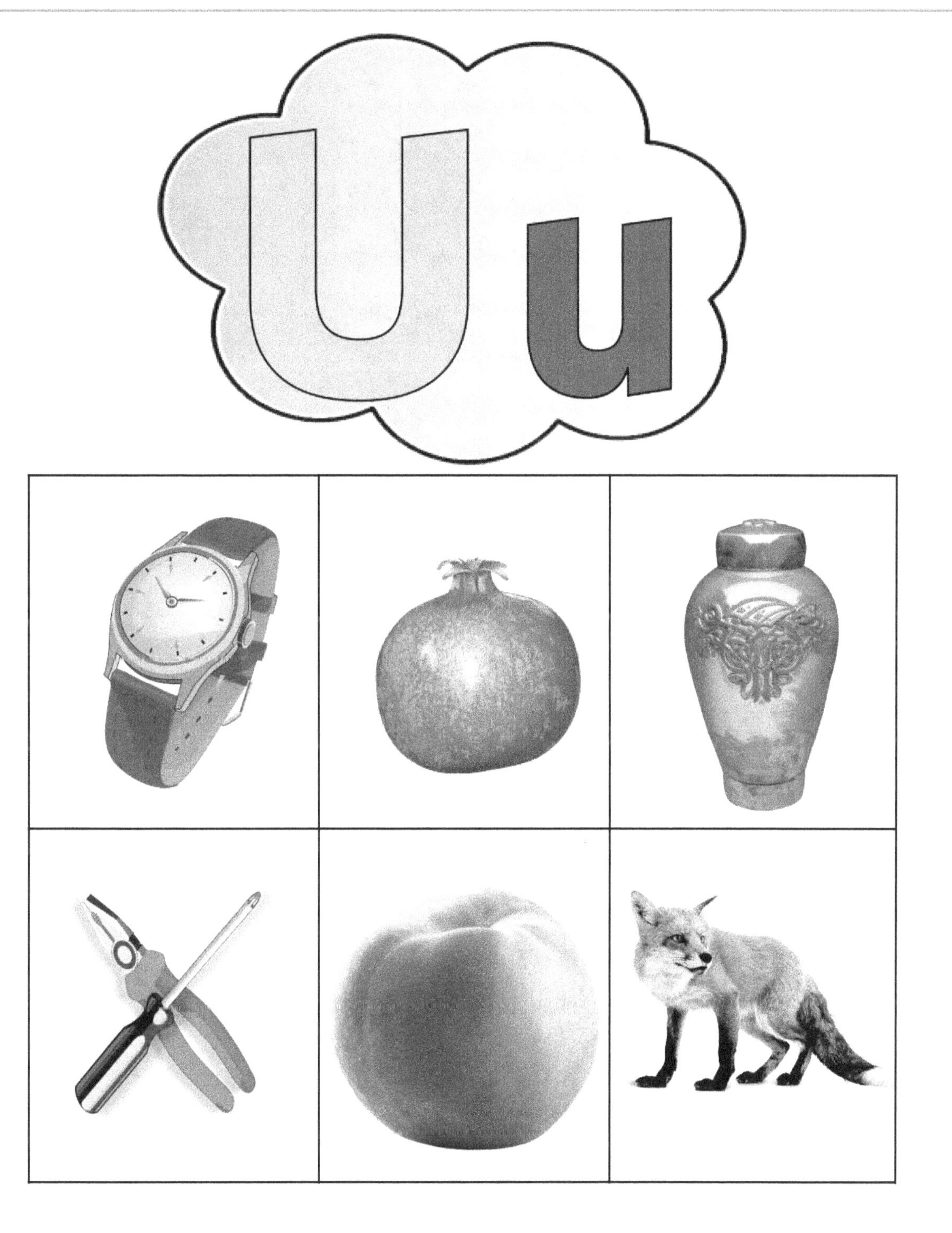

U u

URN

urn

I SPY with my smart eye,
Something beginning with...

V v

VIOLIN

violin

I SPY with my smart eye,
Something beginning with…

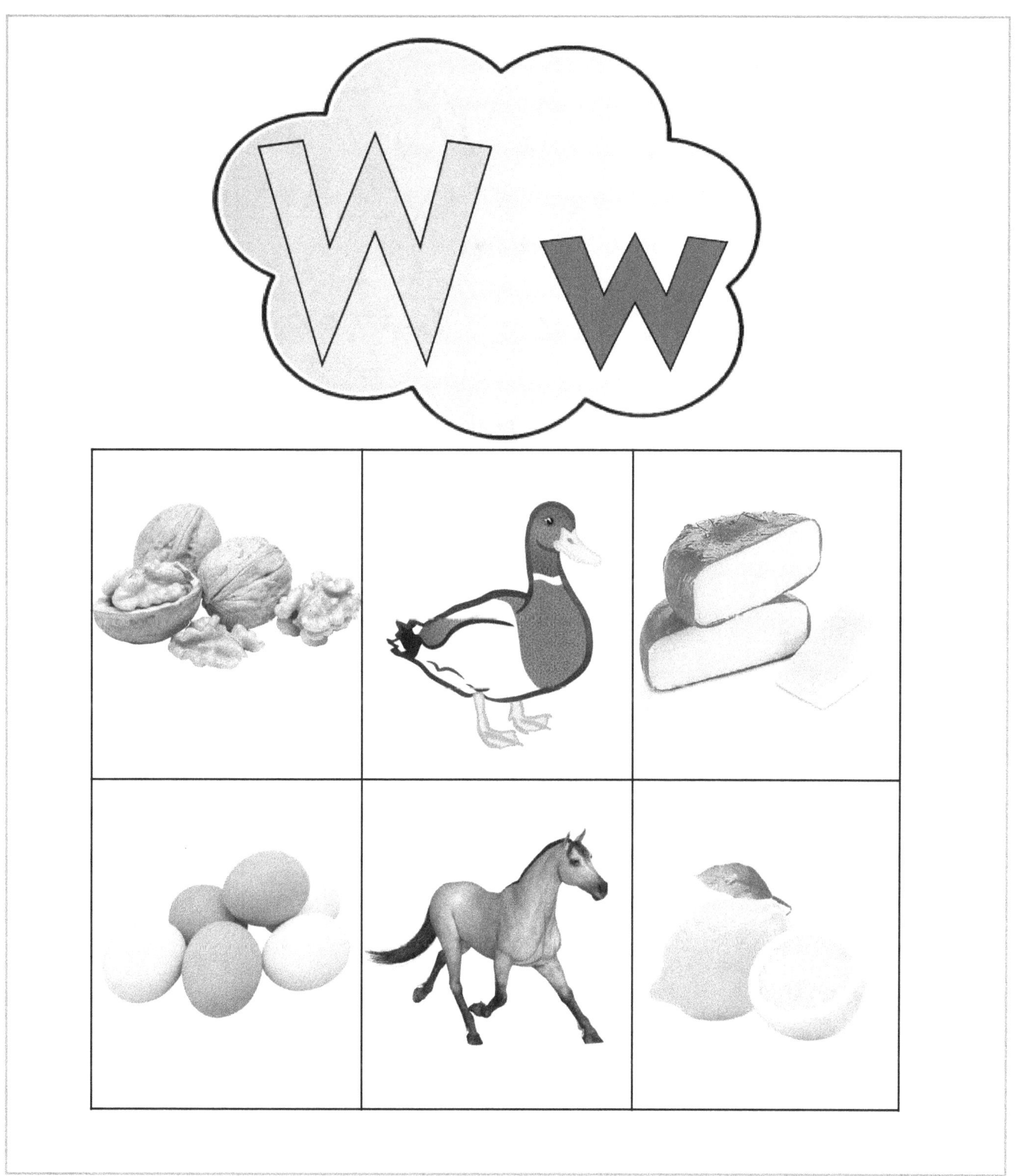

W w

WALNUT

walnut

I SPY with my smart eye, Something beginning with…

X x

XIGUA
xigua

I SPY with my smart eye,
Something beginning with...

Y y

Y y

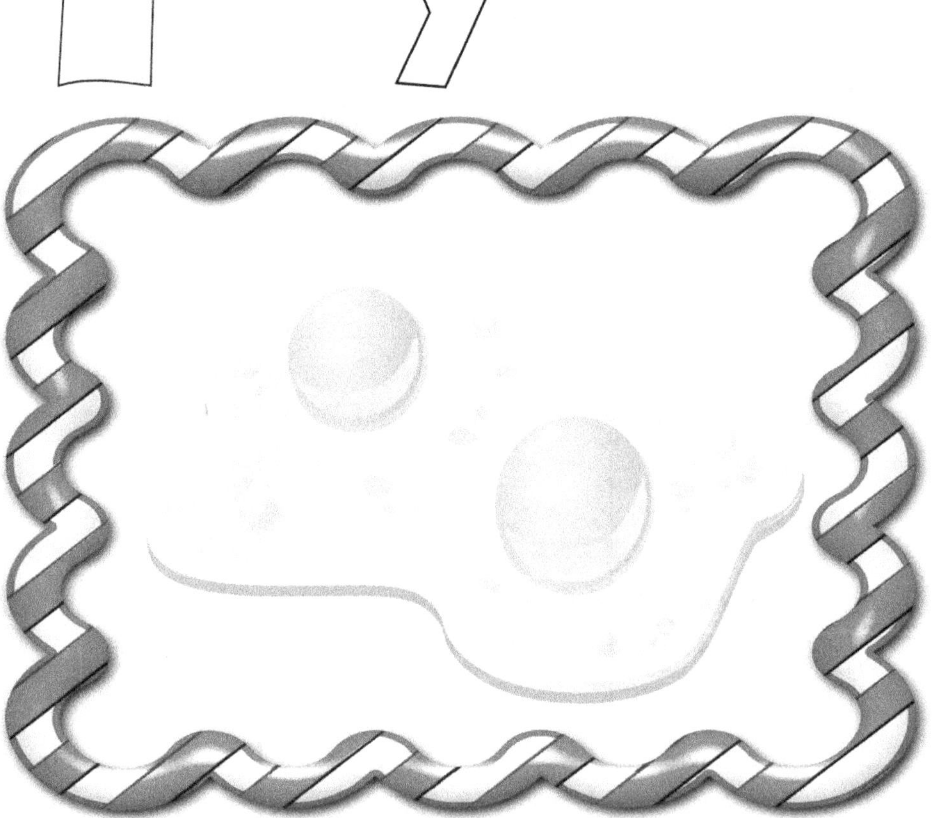

YOLK
yolk

I SPY with my smart eye, Something beginning with…

Z z

ZUCCHINI

zucchini